Breaking Free:
How I Conquered Depression

Franklin Fisher

Published by Amazon KDP

Amazon.com, Inc.

P.O. Box 81226

Seattle, WA 98108-1226

United States.

Printed by Amazon KDP in the USA

Table of Contents

Introduction

At the age of 27, I found myself grappling with the overwhelming darkness of depression. Each day felt like an insurmountable challenge, with simple tasks becoming monumental obstacles. The joy and enthusiasm that once colored my world had faded, leaving me feeling isolated and hopeless. Acknowledging my depression was a difficult and painful process, but it was also the first crucial step toward healing.

Sharing my story is important because it sheds light on the reality of depression, breaking the stigma that often surrounds mental health issues. By opening up about my journey, I hope to encourage others who are struggling to seek help and understand that they are not alone. Everyone's path to recovery is unique, but through shared experiences, we can find strength and solidarity.

Chapter 1.

Acknowledging the Problem

Realization that what you were experiencing was more than temporary sadness

For a long time, I dismissed my feelings as just a phase or a bout of temporary sadness. I attributed my low moods to stress at work, personal challenges, and the ups and downs of everyday life. However, as days turned into weeks and weeks into months, I began to notice a persistent cloud hanging over me. Simple pleasures that once brought me joy no longer had the same effect. My energy levels were perpetually low, and even the most mundane tasks felt like monumental challenges.

I started to realize that this was not just a fleeting period of sadness but something deeper and more entrenched. The constant negative thoughts, the lack of motivation, and the pervasive sense of hopelessness were not things I could simply shake off. This realization was both frightening and enlightening. It marked the beginning of understanding that what I was experiencing was not normal and required attention.

The importance of admitting to yourself that you needed help

Admitting to myself that I needed help was one of the hardest yet most crucial steps in my journey to overcoming depression. For a long time, I battled with feelings of shame and guilt, believing that I should be able to handle my problems on my own. There is a pervasive stigma around mental health that makes it difficult for many to acknowledge their struggles. I, too, fell into the trap of thinking that seeking help was a sign of weakness.

However, as my condition worsened, it became clear that I could not navigate this alone. The turning point came when I realized that admitting I needed help was not a sign of weakness but a courageous step towards healing. This admission required a deep level of self-awareness and honesty. It meant confronting my vulnerabilities and accepting that it was okay to not be okay.

The moment I acknowledged my need for help, a weight lifted off my shoulders. It opened the door to seeking professional assistance and reaching out to those around me. This step was essential because it marked the transition from suffering in silence to actively seeking solutions and support. Acknowledging the problem was the foundation upon which I built my recovery. It allowed me to approach my mental health with the seriousness it deserved and to take proactive steps towards healing.

In retrospect, admitting that I needed help was an act of self-compassion. It was an acknowledgment that my well-being was worth fighting for and that I deserved the support necessary to reclaim my life. This self-acceptance laid the groundwork for the healing process, allowing me to embark on a journey towards recovery with a sense of purpose and hope.

Chapter 2

Seeking Professional Help

Decision to reach out to a therapist

The decision to reach out to a therapist was a pivotal moment in my journey to overcoming depression. For a long time, I resisted the idea of seeking professional help. There were many reasons for my reluctance, including the fear of being judged, the stigma associated with mental health issues, and a misguided belief that I should be able to handle my problems on my own. However, as my depression deepened, it became increasingly clear that I could not navigate this journey alone.

I remember vividly the day I decided to seek help. It was after a particularly difficult week, one in which getting out of bed felt like an insurmountable challenge. The weight of my emotions was becoming unbearable, and I realized that my current coping mechanisms were no longer sufficient. I had reached a point where I needed professional guidance to help me understand and manage my feelings.

The first step in seeking professional help was acknowledging that my mental health was just as important as my physical health. This shift in perspective was crucial. I had always been diligent about visiting a doctor for physical ailments, yet I had neglected my mental well-being. Realizing that seeking help for my mental health was not a sign of weakness but rather an act of self-care was a turning point.

I began by researching therapists in my area. I looked for professionals who specialized in treating depression and had good reviews from their clients. This process was somewhat daunting, but I was determined to find someone who could help me. I also reached out to friends and family for recommendations. Their support and encouragement were invaluable during this time.

Once I had identified a few potential therapists, I made the difficult but necessary step of contacting them. Making that first phone call was incredibly anxiety-inducing. I remember feeling a mix of fear and relief. Fear of the unknown and the vulnerability required to open up about my struggles, but also relief that I was taking an active step towards healing.

My initial consultation with my therapist was a crucial moment. It was an opportunity to gauge whether I felt comfortable with her and whether she could provide the support I needed. During our first session, I was nervous and unsure of what to expect. However, my therapist was warm and understanding, which immediately put me at ease. She explained the therapeutic process and assured me that I was in a safe space where I could express my thoughts and feelings without judgment.

How therapy provided a safe space to express thoughts and feelings

Therapy provided a much-needed safe space for me to express my thoughts and feelings. In my everyday life, I often felt misunderstood or judged when I tried to talk about my depression. Friends and family, despite their best intentions, sometimes struggled to grasp the depth of my feelings. In therapy, however, I found a sanctuary where I could be completely open and honest.

My therapist created an environment of empathy and understanding. She listened attentively to everything I said, validating my experiences and emotions. This validation was incredibly powerful. For the first time in a long while, I felt seen and heard. I didn't have to censor myself or worry about how my words might be received. I could share my darkest thoughts and deepest fears without the fear of rejection or judgment.

One of the most significant aspects of therapy was the opportunity to explore my emotions in a structured way. My therapist used various techniques to help me articulate my feelings. Sometimes, she would ask open-ended questions that encouraged me to delve deeper into my experiences. Other times, she would use specific therapeutic exercises to help me gain clarity. These techniques allowed me to understand my emotions better and to identify patterns in my thoughts and behaviors.

Therapy also provided a space for me to process past traumas and unresolved issues. My therapist helped me explore the underlying causes of my depression. This exploration was not always easy. It required me to confront painful memories and experiences that I had buried deep within myself. However, it was also incredibly healing. By bringing these issues to the surface and addressing them, I was able to start the process of healing old wounds.

Another critical aspect of therapy was the development of coping mechanisms. My therapist taught me various strategies to manage my depression. These strategies included cognitive-behavioral techniques, mindfulness practices, and stress management tools. She also provided practical advice on how to navigate challenging situations in my daily life. These coping mechanisms became invaluable tools in my journey towards recovery.

Learning about underlying issues and coping mechanisms

Through therapy, I began to uncover the underlying issues that were contributing to my depression. This process was like peeling back the layers of an onion. Each session revealed a new layer, bringing me closer to understanding the root causes of my struggles.

One of the first things my therapist helped me realize was the impact of negative thought patterns on my mental health. She introduced me to the concept of cognitive distortions – irrational or biased ways of thinking that can perpetuate negative emotions. Together, we identified several cognitive distortions that I was prone to, such as catastrophizing (expecting the worst-case scenario), black-and-white thinking (viewing situations in extremes), and overgeneralization (drawing broad conclusions from a single event).

By recognizing these cognitive distortions, I was able to challenge and reframe my negative thoughts. My therapist taught me to question the validity of my thoughts and to consider alternative, more balanced perspectives. This process, known as cognitive restructuring, was incredibly empowering. It gave me a sense of control over my thoughts and emotions, which had previously felt overwhelming and uncontrollable.

In addition to addressing cognitive distortions, my therapist helped me explore deeper, more ingrained issues. We delved into my past, examining how my upbringing, relationships, and life experiences had shaped my current mental state. This exploration was often emotional and challenging, but it was also incredibly illuminating. It helped me understand the connections between my past experiences and my present feelings, allowing me to make sense of my emotions in a new way.

One significant revelation was the role of unresolved grief and trauma in my depression. I had experienced several losses and traumatic events in my life that I had never fully processed. My therapist provided a safe space for me to grieve and to confront these traumas. Through this process, I was able to release some of the pain and anger I had been holding onto, which brought a sense of relief and healing.

In addition to uncovering underlying issues, therapy provided me with a range of coping mechanisms to manage my depression. These coping mechanisms became essential tools in my daily life, helping me navigate difficult emotions and situations.

One of the most effective coping mechanisms I learned was mindfulness. Mindfulness involves paying attention to the present moment without judgment. It encourages an attitude of acceptance and curiosity towards one's thoughts and feelings. Through mindfulness practices, such as meditation and deep breathing exercises, I learned to observe my emotions without becoming overwhelmed by them. This practice helped me stay grounded and present, reducing feelings of anxiety and stress.

My therapist also introduced me to various cognitive-behavioral techniques. One such technique was thought challenging, which involves identifying and disputing irrational or unhelpful thoughts. Whenever I noticed a negative thought, I would ask myself questions like, "What evidence do I have that this thought is true?" and "Is there an alternative explanation for this situation?" This process helped me develop a more balanced and realistic perspective.

Another valuable coping mechanism was the use of self-compassion. My therapist encouraged me to treat myself with the same kindness and understanding that I would offer to a friend. This involved recognizing my own suffering, being gentle with myself, and practicing self-care. Self-compassion helped counteract the harsh self-criticism that often accompanied my depression.

In addition to these techniques, my therapist provided practical advice on managing stress and building resilience. She encouraged me to establish a routine that included regular physical activity, healthy eating, and adequate sleep. She also emphasized the importance of social connections and encouraged me to reach out to friends and family for support.

Throughout this process, therapy provided a consistent and supportive environment where I could work through my challenges. My therapist's guidance and expertise were invaluable in helping me navigate my depression. She offered a combination of empathy, insight, and practical tools that empowered me to take control of my mental health.

Conclusion

Seeking professional help was a transformative step in my journey to overcoming depression. The decision to reach out to a therapist marked the beginning of a healing process that involved acknowledging my struggles, exploring underlying issues, and developing effective coping mechanisms. Therapy provided a safe space for me to express my thoughts and feelings, gain insight into my emotions, and learn valuable tools for managing my mental health. Through this process, I emerged stronger, more self-aware, and better equipped to navigate the challenges of life. Seeking help was not a sign of weakness but an act of courage and self-care, and it played a crucial role in my recovery.

Chapter 3

Medication

Initial Apprehension About Taking Antidepressants

When I first considered taking antidepressants, I felt a deep sense of apprehension. There was a swirl of conflicting emotions and thoughts running through my mind. The decision to take medication for my depression was not one that I took lightly. It was a process marked by hesitation, fear, and, ultimately, acceptance.

One of the primary sources of my apprehension was the stigma surrounding mental health medication. Society often places a significant amount of shame on those who need medication for mental health issues. I worried about what people would think if they found out I was taking antidepressants. Would they see me as weak or incapable of handling my problems? This fear of judgment weighed heavily on my decision-making process.

Another major concern was the fear of becoming dependent on medication. I worried that once I started taking antidepressants, I would be reliant on them for the rest of my life. The idea of needing a pill to feel "normal" was unsettling. I feared losing a sense of control over my own mental state and becoming reliant on a pharmaceutical solution.

Additionally, I was concerned about potential side effects. I had heard stories from others about the negative experiences they had with antidepressants – stories of weight gain, loss of libido, insomnia, and emotional numbness. These potential side effects made me wary of starting medication, as I didn't want to trade one set of problems for another.

Despite these concerns, my worsening condition made it clear that I needed more support than therapy alone could provide. My therapist and primary care physician both recommended considering medication as a complementary approach to my treatment. They explained that antidepressants could help stabilize my mood, making it easier for me to engage in therapy and other forms of treatment.

The turning point came when I realized that my quality of life had deteriorated to a point where I needed to take decisive action. My depression was affecting every aspect of my life, from my work to my relationships to my overall well-being. The daily struggle had become too much to bear, and I knew I needed to try something new.

I scheduled an appointment with a psychiatrist to discuss my options. During our consultation, the psychiatrist took the time to address all of my concerns and answer my questions. She explained how antidepressants work, their potential benefits, and the importance of finding the right medication and dosage for my specific needs. This conversation was incredibly reassuring and helped alleviate some of my fears.

With a sense of cautious optimism, I agreed to start a course of antidepressants. My psychiatrist prescribed a selective serotonin reuptake inhibitor (SSRI), one of the most commonly used types of antidepressants. She emphasized that finding the right medication might involve some trial and error and that it could take several weeks to notice any significant changes.

Benefits of Medication in Stabilizing Mood and Enhancing Engagement in Therapy

As I began taking the prescribed antidepressant, I remained vigilant about monitoring my response to the medication. The first few weeks were a period of adjustment. I experienced some mild side effects, such as headaches and slight nausea, but these symptoms were manageable and gradually subsided.

Around the four-week mark, I started to notice a subtle but significant shift in my mood. The pervasive heaviness that had weighed me down for so long began to lift. I found it easier to get out of bed in the morning and felt a glimmer of hope that had been absent for months. This initial improvement was encouraging and motivated me to continue with the medication.

One of the most profound benefits of taking antidepressants was the stabilization of my mood. Before medication, my emotions were like a rollercoaster, with extreme highs and lows that left me feeling exhausted and overwhelmed. The antidepressants helped even out these fluctuations, providing a more consistent emotional baseline. This stability was crucial in helping me navigate daily life with greater ease.

The stabilized mood also had a positive impact on my ability to engage in therapy. Before starting medication, my sessions were often consumed by the intensity of my emotions. While therapy provided valuable insights and coping strategies, it was challenging to fully engage when I felt so overwhelmed. With the help of antidepressants, I was able to approach therapy with a clearer mind and a more balanced emotional state.

In therapy, I could focus more effectively on the underlying issues contributing to my depression. The medication created a mental "breathing room" that allowed me to delve deeper into my thoughts and feelings without being overshadowed by overwhelming sadness or anxiety. This enhanced engagement in therapy led to more productive sessions and accelerated my progress.

Furthermore, the antidepressants helped reduce some of the physical symptoms associated with my depression. Chronic fatigue, difficulty concentrating, and changes in appetite and sleep patterns were all areas where I noticed improvement. With better physical health, I had more energy and motivation to engage in activities that supported my overall well-being, such as exercise, socializing, and pursuing hobbies.

Another significant benefit was the reduction of intrusive negative thoughts. Prior to medication, my mind was often dominated by a constant stream of self-critical and pessimistic thoughts. These thoughts were like a background noise that I couldn't escape, no matter how hard I tried. The antidepressants helped quiet this inner monologue, allowing me to think more clearly and positively.

The combination of medication and therapy also improved my ability to implement coping mechanisms. Techniques such as cognitive-behavioral therapy (CBT), mindfulness, and stress management became more effective when my mood was stabilized. I could practice these strategies with greater consistency and success, reinforcing their benefits over time.

In addition to therapy, medication allowed me to make meaningful lifestyle changes that further supported my recovery. I found it easier to establish a routine, prioritize self-care, and set realistic goals. These positive changes created a reinforcing cycle of improvement, where each step forward built upon the last.

Of course, the journey with antidepressants was not without its challenges. Finding the right medication and dosage took time and required patience. There were moments of doubt and frustration when side effects appeared or when progress seemed slow. However, with the guidance of my psychiatrist and therapist, I was able to navigate these challenges and adjust my treatment plan as needed.

In conclusion, taking antidepressants was a transformative step in my journey to overcoming depression. Despite my initial apprehension, the benefits of medication in stabilizing my mood and enhancing my engagement in therapy were profound. Antidepressants provided the foundation upon which I could build a comprehensive and effective treatment plan, incorporating therapy, coping mechanisms, and lifestyle changes. By addressing the biological aspects of my depression, medication allowed me to regain control of my life and work towards lasting recovery.

Chapter 4

Building a Support System

Importance of Confiding in Friends and Family

The journey through depression can be incredibly isolating. Often, the overwhelming feelings of sadness, hopelessness, and worthlessness make it difficult to reach out to others. However, one of the most crucial steps in my recovery was learning to confide in my friends and family. Opening up to them about my struggles was a turning point that provided me with the support and understanding I desperately needed.

When I first started experiencing the symptoms of depression, I kept my feelings to myself. I was afraid of being judged, misunderstood, or burdening my loved ones with my problems. There was a pervasive stigma surrounding mental health that made me feel ashamed of my condition. I believed that I should be able to handle my issues on my own and that asking for help was a sign of weakness.

However, as my depression deepened, I realized that isolating myself was only making things worse. The burden of carrying my pain alone was becoming unbearable. I needed to break the silence and share my struggles with those closest to me. This realization marked the beginning of a crucial shift in my approach to dealing with depression.

Confiding in friends and family was not easy. It required a great deal of vulnerability and courage. I remember feeling a mix of fear and relief as I prepared to open up. Fear of how they might react, but also relief at the prospect of finally unburdening myself. My first step was to choose a few trusted individuals whom I felt safe confiding in.

I started by talking to my closest friend. We had been through a lot together, and I knew I could trust her with my feelings. One evening, over a quiet dinner, I mustered the courage to share my struggles. I told her about the persistent sadness, the difficulty getting out of bed, and the overwhelming sense of hopelessness. As I spoke, tears welled up in my eyes, and I could see the concern and empathy in her expression.

To my relief, my friend responded with kindness and understanding. She listened without judgment, offering her support and reassurance. She told me that I was not alone and that she was there for me. Her response was a balm to my wounded soul, providing a sense of validation and connection that I had been missing.

Buoyed by this positive experience, I decided to open up to my family. I arranged a meeting with my parents and siblings, explaining that I had something important to discuss. When we sat down together, I shared my struggles with depression, just as I had with my friend. I was honest about how I had been feeling and the impact it was having on my life.

My family's response was one of concern and love. They expressed their support and assured me that they would do whatever they could to help me through this difficult time. Their unconditional love and acceptance were incredibly comforting. It felt like a weight had been lifted off my shoulders, knowing that I had their support.

How Their Support Played a Crucial Role in My Recovery

The support of my friends and family played a pivotal role in my recovery from depression. Their understanding, encouragement, and practical assistance provided a foundation upon which I could build my healing process. Here are several ways in which their support was crucial:

1. **Emotional Support:**
    o Having someone to talk to made a significant difference in my emotional well-being. My friends and family were there to listen when I needed to vent, cry, or simply share my thoughts. They provided a safe space where I could express my feelings without fear of judgment.
    o Their empathy and validation helped me feel understood and less alone. Knowing that they cared about my well-being gave me a sense of comfort and reassurance during the darkest moments of my depression.
2. **Encouragement to Seek Professional Help:**
    o My loved ones encouraged me to seek professional help

when they saw that I was struggling. Their support gave me the courage to reach out to a therapist and consider medication as part of my treatment plan.

- o They helped me navigate the process of finding a therapist, scheduling appointments, and attending sessions. Their encouragement and practical assistance made it easier for me to take these important steps towards recovery.

3. **Practical Assistance:**
    - o Depression often made it difficult for me to manage everyday tasks. My friends and family stepped in to provide practical assistance, such as helping with household chores, running errands, and preparing meals.
    - o Their support in these areas alleviated some of the stress and pressure I was feeling, allowing me to focus on my recovery. Knowing that I had their help made it easier to manage the demands of daily life.

4. **Encouraging Self-Care:**
   - My loved ones encouraged me to prioritize self-care and engage in activities that supported my mental health. They reminded me to take breaks, get enough sleep, eat nutritious meals, and engage in physical activity.
   - They also encouraged me to pursue hobbies and interests that brought me joy and fulfillment. Their encouragement helped me create a balanced and healthy routine that supported my overall well-being.
5. **Providing a Sense of Purpose and Connection:**
   - Depression often left me feeling disconnected and isolated. My friends and family provided a sense of purpose and connection by including me in social activities and family gatherings.
   - Their presence reminded me that I was not alone and that I had people who cared about me. This sense of connection

was a powerful antidote to the feelings of isolation and loneliness that often accompanied my depression.

6. **Offering Perspective and Hope:**
   - During moments of despair, my loved ones offered perspective and hope. They reminded me of my strengths, accomplishments, and the progress I had made in my recovery.
   - Their positive outlook and belief in my ability to overcome depression provided me with a sense of hope and motivation to keep going. Their encouragement helped me stay focused on my goals and continue working towards healing.

7. **Supporting My Treatment Plan:**
   - My friends and family were supportive of my treatment plan, including therapy and medication. They respected my decisions and encouraged me to follow through with my treatment.
   - They also provided accountability by checking in

on my progress and encouraging me to stay committed to my recovery. Their support reinforced the importance of my treatment plan and helped me stay on track.

8. **Offering Unconditional Love:**
    - Perhaps the most important aspect of their support was their unconditional love. They accepted me for who I was, flaws and all, and loved me regardless of my struggles with depression.
    - This unconditional love provided a sense of security and belonging that was essential to my recovery. It reminded me that I was valued and worthy of love, even in my darkest moments.

In conclusion, confiding in my friends and family and receiving their support was a crucial part of my recovery from depression. Their emotional support, encouragement, practical assistance, and unconditional love provided a foundation upon which I could build my healing process. Their presence in my life reminded me that I was not alone and that I had people who cared about my well-being. This sense of connection and support was instrumental in helping me navigate the challenges of depression and work towards lasting recovery.

Chapter 5

Lifestyle Changes for Mental Health

Exercise: The Role of Physical Activity in Improving Mood

Introduction

Physical activity has long been recognized for its benefits to physical health, but its impact on mental health is equally profound. For those dealing with depression, integrating exercise into daily life can be a transformative aspect of the recovery process. This section delves into the various ways in which exercise can improve mood, the mechanisms behind these effects, and practical strategies for incorporating physical activity into a daily routine.

The Psychological Benefits of Exercise

Exercise acts as a powerful tool for improving mood through several psychological mechanisms. One of the most notable is the release of endorphins, the body's natural mood elevators. Endorphins are neurotransmitters that interact with the opiate receptors in the brain to reduce the perception of pain and produce a positive feeling in the body. This phenomenon, often referred to as the "runner's high," can create a temporary boost in mood and energy.

Additionally, exercise promotes the release of other chemicals, such as serotonin and dopamine. These neurotransmitters play a crucial role in regulating mood, and their increased production through physical activity can help counteract feelings of sadness and depression. Studies have shown that regular exercise can be as effective as antidepressant medications for some individuals, highlighting its importance as a complementary treatment for depression.

Moreover, exercise can help reduce stress. Physical activity lowers the levels of the body's stress hormones, such as cortisol, and stimulates the production of endorphins. This reduction in stress can lead to improved mental health and a better overall mood.

Exercise as a Distraction from Negative Thoughts

One of the challenges of depression is the prevalence of negative thoughts and rumination. Exercise can serve as a productive distraction from these negative thought patterns. Engaging in physical activity requires focus and concentration, which can shift attention away from distressing thoughts and provide a mental break from the cycle of negativity.

For example, going for a walk, joining a fitness class, or playing a sport demands attention to the physical activity itself, as well as the immediate environment. This focus can provide a temporary escape from the internal struggles of depression and help individuals feel more present and engaged in the moment.

Building a Sustainable Exercise Routine

Starting an exercise routine can be challenging, especially for those dealing with depression. One of the keys to success is to create a routine that is both manageable and enjoyable. Here are some strategies to build and maintain a sustainable exercise routine:

1. **Set Realistic Goals:** Begin with small, achievable goals to build confidence and establish a habit. For example, start with a 10-minute walk each day and gradually increase the

duration and intensity as you become more comfortable.

2. **Choose Activities You Enjoy:** Engage in physical activities that you find enjoyable. Whether it's dancing, swimming, hiking, or cycling, finding pleasure in the exercise itself can increase motivation and adherence.

3. **Incorporate Exercise into Your Daily Routine:** Schedule exercise at a time of day that works best for you. Whether it's in the morning, during lunch breaks, or in the evening, consistency is crucial for establishing a routine.

4. **Find a Workout Buddy:** Exercising with a friend or joining a group can provide social support and accountability. This can make the process more enjoyable and help you stick to your routine.

5. **Track Your Progress:** Keep a journal or use a fitness app to track your workouts and monitor your progress. This can help you stay motivated and recognize the benefits of your efforts.

6. **Be Patient with Yourself:** Understand that building a new habit takes time. There will be days when you may not feel like exercising, and

that's okay. The important thing is to get back on track and keep moving forward.

The Long-Term Impact of Regular Exercise

The long-term benefits of regular exercise extend beyond immediate mood improvements. Consistent physical activity can lead to sustained mental health benefits, including:

1. **Improved Self-Esteem:** As you achieve fitness goals and notice physical changes, your self-esteem and body image can improve. This boost in self-confidence can contribute to better mental health.
2. **Better Stress Management:** Regular exercise can improve your ability to manage stress. By incorporating physical activity into your routine, you develop a healthier way to cope with stress and anxiety.
3. **Enhanced Cognitive Function:** Exercise has been shown to improve cognitive functions such as memory, attention, and executive function. These cognitive benefits can help you

better manage depression and improve your overall mental clarity.

4. **Increased Resilience:** The discipline of maintaining an exercise routine can build resilience and determination. This sense of accomplishment and perseverance can be applied to other areas of life, supporting overall mental health and well-being.

Diet: Importance of a Nutritious Diet for Mental Health

Introduction

Diet plays a significant role in mental health, impacting everything from mood regulation to cognitive function. A balanced and nutritious diet supports mental health by providing essential nutrients that the brain and body need to function optimally. This section explores the connection between diet and mental health, highlighting the importance of nutrition in managing depression and offering practical advice for making healthier food choices.

The Link Between Nutrition and Mental Health

Nutrition is closely linked to mental health through various biological mechanisms. The brain requires a wide range of nutrients to maintain its structure and function, and deficiencies in these nutrients can contribute to mental health issues, including depression.

1. **Nutrients and Brain Function:**
   - **Omega-3 Fatty Acids:** These essential fats, found in fish like salmon and in flaxseeds and walnuts, are crucial for brain health. Omega-3 fatty acids are components of cell membranes and play a role in neurotransmitter function and inflammation reduction. Studies have shown that omega-3 supplementation can improve symptoms of depression.
   - **B Vitamins:** B vitamins, including B6, B12, and folate, are vital for neurotransmitter synthesis and function. Deficiencies in these vitamins can lead to mood disorders and cognitive decline. Foods rich in B vitamins include leafy greens, legumes, and fortified cereals.

- o **Vitamin D:** Often referred to as the "sunshine vitamin," vitamin D is important for mood regulation and brain health. Low levels of vitamin D have been associated with depression, and sunlight exposure or supplementation can help maintain adequate levels.
- o **Magnesium:** This mineral supports numerous biochemical reactions in the body, including those related to mood regulation. Magnesium-rich foods include nuts, seeds, whole grains, and green leafy vegetables.

2. **The Role of Blood Sugar Regulation:**
   - o Stable blood sugar levels are crucial for maintaining energy and mood. Consuming foods that cause rapid spikes and crashes in blood sugar can lead to mood swings and irritability. A diet rich in complex carbohydrates, such as whole grains, fruits, and

vegetables, helps regulate blood sugar levels.

3. **The Gut-Brain Connection:**
    o   Emerging research highlights the connection between gut health and mental health. The gut microbiome, the community of microorganisms in the digestive tract, influences brain function and mood. A diet high in fiber, prebiotics, and probiotics supports a healthy gut microbiome and may reduce symptoms of depression.

Creating a Nutritious Diet for Mental Health

Adopting a nutritious diet can be an effective strategy for managing depression. Here are some practical tips for creating a diet that supports mental health:

1. **Focus on Whole Foods:** Prioritize whole, unprocessed foods in your diet. These foods are rich in essential nutrients and free from the additives and sugars found in processed foods. Examples of whole foods include

fruits, vegetables, whole grains, lean proteins, and healthy fats.

2. **Incorporate a Variety of Foods:** A diverse diet ensures that you get a wide range of nutrients. Include a variety of fruits and vegetables, different protein sources (such as beans, fish, and poultry), and whole grains in your meals.

3. **Plan Balanced Meals:** Aim for balanced meals that include a combination of carbohydrates, proteins, and fats. This balance helps stabilize blood sugar levels and provides sustained energy. For example, a meal might consist of grilled chicken, quinoa, and a side of mixed vegetables.

4. **Stay Hydrated:** Hydration is essential for overall health, including mental health. Drinking enough water throughout the day supports brain function and can improve mood and cognitive performance.

5. **Limit Sugary and Processed Foods:** Reducing the intake of sugary snacks, sodas, and processed foods can prevent blood sugar spikes and crashes that affect mood. Opt for healthier snacks like nuts, yogurt, or fruit.

6. **Mindful Eating:** Practice mindful eating by paying attention to your hunger and fullness cues. Eating slowly and savoring your food can improve digestion and help you make healthier food choices.

The Long-Term Benefits of a Nutritious Diet

Maintaining a nutritious diet offers long-term benefits for mental health and overall well-being. These benefits extend beyond the immediate effects of eating well and contribute to sustained mental health improvements.

1. **Improved Mood Stability:** A balanced diet helps regulate mood by providing essential nutrients that support neurotransmitter function and blood sugar stability. Over time, these dietary habits can lead to a more stable and positive mood.
2. **Enhanced Cognitive Function:** Consuming a diet rich in brain-boosting nutrients supports cognitive functions such as memory, focus, and problem-solving. Long-term adherence to a nutritious diet can

contribute to better mental clarity and cognitive health.

3. **Reduced Risk of Mental Health Issues:** A healthy diet can lower the risk of developing mental health conditions. Nutrient-rich foods can support brain health and reduce inflammation, which may decrease the likelihood of future mood disorders.

4. **Increased Energy Levels:** A well-rounded diet provides the necessary energy for daily activities. Improved energy levels can enhance motivation and engagement in both physical and mental health activities.

Sleep: Establishing a Regular Sleep Routine

Introduction

Sleep is a fundamental aspect of mental health that is often overlooked in discussions about depression and recovery. Establishing a regular sleep routine can have profound effects on mood, energy levels, and overall mental well-being. This section explores the importance of sleep for mental health, the impact of sleep disturbances on depression, and practical strategies for creating a consistent sleep routine.

The Importance of Sleep for Mental Health

Sleep plays a critical role in mental health and emotional regulation. Adequate sleep is essential for brain function, emotional balance, and overall mental well-being.

1. **Mood Regulation:** Quality sleep is essential for mood regulation. During sleep, the brain processes emotional experiences and consolidates memories. Poor sleep can disrupt this process, leading to increased irritability, mood swings, and depressive symptoms.
2. **Cognitive Function:** Sleep is crucial for cognitive functions such as attention, memory, and problem-solving. Sleep deprivation can impair cognitive performance and exacerbate symptoms of depression.
3. **Stress Reduction:** Adequate sleep helps regulate stress hormones, such as cortisol. Poor sleep can lead to elevated cortisol levels, which can contribute to feelings of anxiety and depression.

4. **Emotional Resilience:** A good night's sleep enhances emotional resilience, helping individuals better cope with stress and challenges. This increased resilience can support mental health and recovery from depression.

The Impact of Sleep Disturbances on Depression

Sleep disturbances are both a symptom and a contributing factor to depression. Understanding this relationship is crucial for developing effective strategies for managing depression through sleep.

1. **Insomnia:** Insomnia, characterized by difficulty falling or staying asleep, is a common symptom of depression. Chronic insomnia can exacerbate depressive symptoms and create a vicious cycle of poor sleep and worsening mood.
2. **Hypersomnia:** Conversely, hypersomnia, or excessive sleeping, can also be a sign of depression. While it may seem like a form of self-care, excessive sleep can contribute to a lack of motivation and hinder recovery from depression.

3. **Sleep Architecture Changes:** Depression can alter sleep architecture, affecting the quality of sleep. Changes in sleep patterns, such as reduced REM sleep or fragmented sleep, can impact mental health and mood regulation.

Strategies for Establishing a Regular Sleep Routine

Creating a consistent sleep routine involves several practical steps that can help improve sleep quality and support mental health. Here are some effective strategies:

1. **Set a Consistent Sleep Schedule:** Go to bed and wake up at the same times every day, even on weekends. This consistency helps regulate your internal clock and promotes better sleep.
2. **Create a Relaxing Bedtime Routine:** Develop a calming pre-sleep routine to signal to your body that it's time to wind down. Activities might include reading a book, taking a warm bath, or practicing relaxation techniques such as deep breathing or meditation.

3. **Optimize Your Sleep Environment:** Ensure your sleep environment is conducive to rest. This includes maintaining a comfortable mattress, keeping the room dark and quiet, and maintaining a cool temperature.

4. **Limit Exposure to Screens Before Bed:** The blue light emitted by screens can interfere with melatonin production, making it harder to fall asleep. Avoid screens for at least an hour before bedtime and consider using blue light filters if screen use is necessary.

5. **Be Mindful of Food and Drink:** Avoid large meals, caffeine, and alcohol close to bedtime. These substances can disrupt sleep patterns and affect the quality of your rest.

6. **Incorporate Physical Activity:** Regular exercise can improve sleep quality, but try to complete physical activity at least a few hours before bedtime. Exercising too close to bedtime can make it harder to fall asleep.

7. **Manage Stress and Anxiety:** Addressing stress and anxiety through techniques such as mindfulness, journaling, or talking to

a therapist can improve sleep quality and support mental health.

The Long-Term Benefits of a Consistent Sleep Routine

Maintaining a regular sleep routine offers long-term benefits for mental health and overall well-being. These benefits extend beyond immediate improvements in sleep quality and can contribute to sustained mental health.

1. **Improved Mood:** A consistent sleep routine helps regulate mood and reduce symptoms of depression. Better sleep leads to more balanced emotions and improved resilience to stress.
2. **Enhanced Cognitive Function:** Regular, high-quality sleep supports cognitive functions such as memory, attention, and problem-solving. This cognitive support can aid in managing depression and improving overall mental clarity.
3. **Better Stress Management:** Adequate sleep helps regulate stress hormones and supports emotional resilience. A consistent sleep routine

can improve your ability to cope with stress and maintain mental health.

4. **Increased Energy and Motivation:** Quality sleep boosts energy levels and motivation. Improved sleep can lead to greater engagement in daily activities, including those that support mental health and recovery.

Conclusion

Lifestyle changes play a critical role in managing depression and supporting mental health. Exercise, diet, and sleep are three foundational aspects of a healthy lifestyle that can significantly impact mood, cognitive function, and overall well-being.

Exercise offers psychological benefits such as the release of mood-enhancing chemicals, serves as a distraction from negative thoughts, and supports long-term mental health improvements. By setting realistic goals, finding enjoyable activities, and building a sustainable routine, individuals can harness the power of physical activity to support their mental health.

Diet influences mental health through its impact on brain function, blood sugar regulation, and the gut-brain connection. A nutritious diet that includes a variety of whole foods, balanced meals, and mindful eating practices can support mood stability, cognitive function, and overall mental well-being.

Sleep is essential for mood regulation, cognitive function, and stress management. Establishing a regular sleep routine, optimizing the sleep environment, and addressing sleep disturbances can lead to long-term mental health benefits and support the recovery process.

By integrating these lifestyle changes into daily life, individuals can create a solid foundation for managing depression and promoting mental health. Each of these aspects—exercise, diet, and sleep—interconnects to support overall well-being, and together they form a comprehensive approach to mental health that goes beyond immediate relief to foster lasting recovery and resilience.

These references offer additional information and research on the topics covered in the discussion of exercise, diet, and sleep in relation to mental health.

This extensive overview provides a detailed examination of how exercise, diet, and sleep contribute to mental health and offers practical advice for making effective lifestyle changes.

Chapter 6

Mindfulness and Meditation

Introduction

Mindfulness and meditation have emerged as powerful practices for improving mental health and well-being. These techniques offer individuals a way to manage stress, enhance emotional resilience, and cultivate a sense of inner peace. For those dealing with mental health challenges, such as depression or anxiety, integrating mindfulness and meditation into daily life can provide significant benefits. This extensive exploration delves into the practice of mindfulness and meditation, offering practical guidance for incorporating these techniques into your routine and exploring the myriad benefits of staying grounded and present.

Incorporation of Mindfulness and Meditation into Daily Routine

1. Understanding Mindfulness and Meditation

Mindfulness is the practice of being fully present and engaged in the current moment. It involves paying attention to your thoughts, feelings, and surroundings without judgment. Mindfulness encourages you to observe your experiences as they are, fostering a sense of awareness and acceptance.

Meditation is a broad term for various techniques designed to promote mental clarity, emotional balance, and spiritual growth. While there are many forms of meditation, most practices involve focusing attention, calming the mind, and developing a deeper connection to oneself.

2. Starting with Mindfulness

a. Setting Intentions for Mindfulness

Before you begin practicing mindfulness, it's important to set clear intentions. Ask yourself why you want to cultivate mindfulness in your life. Your reasons might include reducing stress, improving focus, or developing greater emotional awareness. Setting intentions helps guide your practice and gives you a sense of purpose.

b. Mindful Breathing

One of the simplest ways to start practicing mindfulness is through mindful breathing. This technique involves paying attention to your breath and observing the sensations of inhalation and exhalation.

Steps for Mindful Breathing:

1. Find a quiet and comfortable place to sit.
2. Close your eyes and take a few deep breaths.
3. Focus on the sensation of your breath entering and leaving your body.
4. When your mind wanders, gently bring your attention back to your breath.
5. Practice for 5–10 minutes daily, gradually increasing the duration as you become more comfortable.

c. Mindful Observation

Mindful observation involves paying close attention to your environment. This practice helps you connect with the present moment through your senses.

Steps for Mindful Observation:

1. Choose an object or scene to focus on, such as a flower, a tree, or a piece of artwork.
2. Observe the details of the object, noting colors, shapes, and textures.
3. Pay attention to any sensations or feelings that arise as you observe.
4. Practice this exercise for a few minutes each day, using it as a break from your routine.

d. Mindful Eating

Mindful eating encourages you to fully engage with the experience of eating. It involves paying attention to the flavors, textures, and sensations of food.

Steps for Mindful Eating:

1. Sit down at the table and take a moment to appreciate your meal.
2. Eat slowly, savoring each bite.
3. Notice the taste, texture, and aroma of the food.
4. Pay attention to your hunger and fullness cues.
5. Practice mindful eating during one meal or snack each day.

3. Incorporating Meditation into Your Routine

a. Choosing a Meditation Practice

There are many types of meditation, so it's important to find one that resonates with you. Some popular meditation practices include:

- **Guided Meditation:** Uses recordings or apps to lead you through meditation sessions.
- **Mindfulness Meditation:** Focuses on being present and aware of thoughts and sensations.
- **Loving-Kindness Meditation:** Cultivates compassion and empathy towards yourself and others.
- **Body Scan Meditation:** Guides you through a systematic focus on different parts of the body to promote relaxation.

b. Establishing a Meditation Routine

Creating a regular meditation practice involves setting aside dedicated time each day.

Steps for Establishing a Routine:

1. **Choose a Time:** Decide on a specific time each day for meditation. It could be in the morning, during lunch, or before bed.
2. **Find a Comfortable Space:** Create a calm and quiet environment for meditation. Use a chair, cushion, or floor space where you can sit comfortably.
3. **Start Small:** Begin with short meditation sessions, such as 5–10 minutes. Gradually increase the duration as you become more comfortable.
4. **Use Resources:** Consider using meditation apps or guided recordings to help you get started. Apps like Headspace, Calm, or Insight Timer offer a variety of guided meditations.
5. **Be Consistent:** Consistency is key to developing a meditation habit. Try to meditate at the same time each day to establish a routine.

c. Exploring Different Techniques

Experiment with different meditation techniques to find what works best for you.

Examples of Techniques:

- **Breath Awareness:** Focus on your breath as it flows in and out.
- **Mantra Meditation:** Repeat a word or phrase to focus your mind.
- **Visualization:** Picture a peaceful scene or imagine a calming place.
- **Body Scan:** Pay attention to physical sensations in different parts of your body.

4. Overcoming Challenges

a. Dealing with Distractions

It's normal for your mind to wander during meditation. When this happens, gently bring your focus back to your practice.

b. Managing Time Constraints

If you're struggling to find time for mindfulness or meditation, look for small opportunities throughout your day. Even a few minutes of practice can be beneficial.

c. Staying Motivated

Keep your practice enjoyable and rewarding. Reflect on the benefits you're experiencing and consider joining a meditation group or community for support.

5. Building a Mindfulness and Meditation Practice

a. Setting Realistic Goals

Set achievable goals for your mindfulness and meditation practice. Goals might include meditating for a certain number of days each week or exploring new techniques.

b. Tracking Your Progress

Keep a journal to track your mindfulness and meditation practice. Note the techniques you're using, the time spent, and any observations or insights.

c. Reflecting on Your Experience

Periodically reflect on your practice to assess its impact on your mental health and well-being. Consider how mindfulness and meditation are affecting your stress levels, mood, and overall life satisfaction.

d. Adapting Your Practice

Be open to adapting your practice as needed. If you find that a certain technique isn't working for you, try a different approach or adjust your routine.

Benefits of Staying Grounded and Present

1. Reducing Stress and Anxiety

a. Mindfulness and Stress Reduction

Mindfulness can help reduce stress by encouraging you to focus on the present moment rather than worrying about the past or future. This practice helps break the cycle of stress and anxiety by promoting a sense of calm and relaxation.

b. Techniques for Stress Management

- **Mindful Breathing:** Focus on your breath to center yourself and reduce stress.
- **Body Scan:** Acknowledge and release physical tension in your body.
- **Mindful Walking:** Engage with your environment during a walk to shift focus from stressors.

c. Long-Term Benefits

Consistent mindfulness practice can lead to long-term stress reduction and improved emotional resilience. Over time, mindfulness can help you develop healthier responses to stress and manage anxiety more effectively.

2. Enhancing Emotional Resilience

a. Emotional Awareness

Mindfulness and meditation help you become more aware of your emotions and their triggers. By observing your emotions without judgment, you can develop a more balanced and accepting attitude toward them.

b. Building Resilience Through Practice

Regular practice of mindfulness and meditation fosters emotional resilience. This resilience allows you to navigate difficult emotions and situations with greater ease.

c. Benefits of Emotional Resilience

Emotional resilience helps you handle setbacks and challenges with a positive mindset. It supports mental health by promoting emotional stability and encouraging constructive coping strategies.

3. Improving Focus and Concentration

a. The Impact of Mindfulness on Cognitive Function

Mindfulness improves cognitive functions such as attention, focus, and memory. By training your mind to remain present, you enhance your ability to concentrate and engage in tasks more effectively.

b. Techniques for Improving Focus

- **Mindful Meditation:** Practice focusing on a single object or thought.
- **Attention Training:** Engage in activities that challenge and strengthen your attention span.
- **Mindful Tasks:** Perform daily tasks with full awareness and attention.

c. Long-Term Cognitive Benefits

Over time, regular mindfulness practice can lead to lasting improvements in cognitive function. Enhanced focus and concentration contribute to better performance in personal and professional life.

4. Fostering a Sense of Inner Peace

a. Cultivating Inner Calm

Mindfulness and meditation help cultivate a sense of inner peace by encouraging you to let go of worries and embrace the present moment. This sense of calm supports mental health and well-being.

b. Techniques for Finding Inner Peace

- **Loving-Kindness Meditation:** Practice sending positive thoughts and feelings to yourself and others.
- **Visualization:** Imagine a peaceful and serene place to promote relaxation.
- **Gratitude Practice:** Reflect on the positive aspects of your life to foster a sense of contentment.

c. Benefits of Inner Peace

A sense of inner peace supports overall mental health and well-being. It provides a foundation for coping with stress and maintaining emotional balance.

5. Developing Greater Self-Awareness

a. Mindfulness as a Tool for Self-Discovery

Mindfulness encourages self-awareness by helping you observe your thoughts, feelings, and behaviors. This self-awareness supports personal growth and self-improvement.

b. Techniques for Enhancing Self-Awareness

- **Journaling:** Write about your thoughts and feelings to gain insights.
- **Self-Reflection:** Reflect on your experiences and how they affect you.
- **Mindful Inquiry:** Ask yourself questions about your reactions and behaviors.

c. The Benefits of Self-Awareness

Greater self-awareness supports personal growth and helps you understand your motivations and responses. It enhances your ability to make informed decisions and cultivate meaningful relationships.

6. Strengthening Relationships

a. Mindfulness in Interactions

Mindfulness improves relationships by encouraging active listening and empathetic communication. Being present in conversations helps you connect with others on a deeper level.

b. Techniques for Strengthening Relationships

- **Active Listening:** Focus fully on the speaker and respond thoughtfully.
- **Empathy Practice:** Try to understand others' perspectives and feelings.
- **Mindful Communication:** Communicate with awareness and intention.

c. Benefits of Strong Relationships

Healthy relationships are essential for mental health and well-being. Mindfulness and meditation support the development of meaningful connections and foster supportive social networks.

Conclusion

Incorporating mindfulness and meditation into your daily routine offers numerous benefits for mental health and well-being. These practices help you stay grounded and present, offering tools for stress management, emotional resilience, and personal growth.

By starting with simple mindfulness techniques and exploring various forms of meditation, you can develop a consistent practice that supports your mental health journey. Over time, these practices can lead to lasting improvements in stress levels, emotional resilience, focus, and overall life satisfaction.

Summary of Benefits:

- **Stress Reduction:** Mindfulness helps manage stress and anxiety by promoting present-moment awareness.
- **Emotional Resilience:** Regular practice fosters emotional stability and resilience.
- **Improved Focus:** Mindfulness enhances cognitive functions such as concentration and memory.
- **Inner Peace:** Meditation cultivates a sense of calm and contentment.
- **Self-Awareness:** Mindfulness encourages self-discovery and personal growth.
- **Strengthened Relationships:** Mindfulness improves communication and empathy in relationships.

Chapter 7

Setting Realistic Goals

Introduction

Setting goals is a fundamental aspect of personal and professional development. Effective goal-setting helps individuals stay motivated, track progress, and achieve success. However, the process of setting goals can be challenging. Many people struggle with creating goals that are realistic and attainable, which can lead to frustration and discouragement. This comprehensive guide explores the principles of setting realistic goals and the importance of celebrating small victories. By the end, you will have a thorough understanding of how to set achievable goals and maintain motivation through acknowledging your progress.

1. Understanding Realistic Goals

a. What Are Realistic Goals?

Realistic goals are those that are achievable within a specific timeframe and with the resources available to you. They are neither too ambitious nor too trivial. Realistic goals strike a balance between being challenging enough to motivate you and being achievable enough to prevent frustration.

b. Characteristics of Realistic Goals

To be considered realistic, a goal should have the following characteristics:

- **Specific:** Clearly defined and unambiguous. For example, "I want to improve my fitness" is too vague, whereas "I want to go to the gym three times a week for the next three months" is specific.
- **Measurable:** Quantifiable so that you can track progress. For instance, "I want to save $500 in three months" is measurable, whereas "I want to save money" is not.
- **Achievable:** Attainable given your current resources, skills, and time constraints. Setting a goal like "I want to run a marathon in a month" might be unrealistic if you are new to running.
- **Relevant:** Aligned with your long-term objectives and values. For example, if you aim to improve your health, setting a goal to eat more vegetables is relevant.

- **Time-Bound:** Has a clear deadline or timeframe. A goal should have a start and end date to create a sense of urgency and structure.

c. The Importance of Realistic Goals

Realistic goals are crucial for several reasons:

- **Motivation:** Realistic goals keep you motivated as you can see progress and are less likely to feel overwhelmed.
- **Clarity:** They provide clear direction and a roadmap for what you need to achieve.
- **Achievement:** They increase the likelihood of success, which builds confidence and encourages you to set new goals.

2. Learning to Set Achievable Goals

a. Assessing Your Current Situation

Before setting a goal, evaluate your current situation to understand what you can realistically achieve. This involves:

- **Identifying Strengths and Weaknesses:** Reflect on your skills, resources, and limitations.

Understanding your strengths can help you set ambitious yet achievable goals, while recognizing your weaknesses can guide you to set more feasible objectives.

- **Analyzing Past Experiences:** Review your past goals and their outcomes. Identify what worked, what didn't, and why. This reflection can provide insights into how to set more realistic goals in the future.

b. Breaking Down Goals into Smaller Steps

Large goals can seem daunting, but breaking them down into smaller, manageable steps makes them more achievable.

Steps for Breaking Down Goals:

1. **Define the End Goal:** Clearly articulate your main objective.

   Example: "I want to write a book."

2. **Identify Major Milestones:** Break the end goal into significant phases.

   Example: "Research, Outline, Write Draft, Edit, Publish."

3. **Create Smaller Tasks:** For each milestone, list smaller tasks required to achieve it.

   Example for "Research": "Read relevant books, Find sources, Take notes."

4. **Assign Deadlines:** Set deadlines for each task and milestone.

   Example: "Complete research by the end of the month."

c. Utilizing the SMART Framework

The SMART framework is a popular method for setting effective goals.

- **Specific:** Define what you want to achieve.
- **Measurable:** Determine how you will measure success.
- **Achievable:** Ensure that your goal is realistic.
- **Relevant:** Align your goal with your larger objectives.
- **Time-Bound:** Set a deadline for completion.

Examples of SMART Goals:

- **Specific:** "I will improve my public speaking skills."
- **Measurable:** "I will attend a public speaking workshop and practice once a week."
- **Achievable:** "I will start with basic workshops and gradually seek more advanced opportunities."
- **Relevant:** "Improving my public speaking will help advance my career."
- **Time-Bound:** "I will complete the workshop and practice for six months."

d. Setting Short-Term vs. Long-Term Goals

It's essential to distinguish between short-term and long-term goals.

- **Short-Term Goals:** Achievable in the near future, usually within a few weeks or months. Example: "Complete a one-week online course."
- **Long-Term Goals:** Require more time to achieve, often several months or years. Example: "Earn a degree in a specific field."

Both types of goals are important for overall success. Short-term goals help you make consistent progress, while long-term goals provide a vision for the future.

e. Setting Personal and Professional Goals

Goals can be categorized into personal and professional spheres.

- **Personal Goals:** Focus on self-improvement and life satisfaction. Examples include improving health, learning a new hobby, or developing better relationships.
- **Professional Goals:** Centered on career advancement and job satisfaction. Examples include achieving a promotion, acquiring new skills, or completing a significant project.

f. Balancing Multiple Goals

Managing multiple goals requires prioritization and effective time management.

- **Identify Priorities:** Determine which goals are most important and align with your values.

- **Create a Balanced Plan:** Allocate time and resources to each goal without spreading yourself too thin.
- **Adjust as Needed:** Be flexible and adjust your plans based on progress and changing circumstances.

3. Celebrating Small Victories to Build Confidence

a. The Importance of Celebrating Success

Celebrating small victories is vital for maintaining motivation and building confidence.

- **Acknowledge Progress:** Recognizing achievements reinforces positive behavior and motivates you to continue working toward your goals.
- **Boosts Morale:** Celebrations create a sense of accomplishment and satisfaction.
- **Strengthens Commitment:** Celebrating milestones can reaffirm your commitment to long-term goals.

b. Strategies for Celebrating Achievements

1. Acknowledging Achievements:

Recognize and reflect on what you've accomplished. Take time to appreciate the effort you put in and the progress you made.

- **Journaling:** Write about your achievements and what they mean to you.
- **Sharing Success:** Talk about your accomplishments with friends, family, or colleagues.

2. Rewarding Yourself:

Rewards can be a great way to celebrate success and reinforce positive behavior.

- **Treat Yourself:** Enjoy a small treat, such as a favorite meal or a day off.
- **Gift:** Buy yourself something meaningful as a reward.
- **Celebrate:** Plan a small celebration or outing to mark your achievement.

3. Reflecting on Your Journey:

Reflect on the steps you took to reach your goal and the lessons learned along the way.

- **Self-Reflection:** Consider what you did well and what you might improve for future goals.
- **Document Success:** Keep a record of your achievements and what you learned from them.

4. Setting New Goals:

Use your success as a springboard for setting new, more ambitious goals.

- **Evaluate Your Goals:** Reflect on your current goals and set new ones based on your achievements.
- **Plan Next Steps:** Create a plan for your next set of goals and how you will achieve them.

c. Overcoming the Fear of Failure

Celebrating small victories can help overcome the fear of failure and build resilience.

- **Reframe Failure:** View setbacks as opportunities for growth and learning.
- **Focus on Effort:** Recognize that effort and persistence are valuable, regardless of the outcome.

- **Seek Support:** Talk to others about your fears and seek advice or encouragement.

d. Creating a Goal-Achievement System

Develop a system for tracking your progress and celebrating achievements.

- **Goal Tracker:** Use a planner, app, or journal to track your progress and milestones.
- **Achievement Log:** Keep a log of your accomplishments and rewards.
- **Review and Reflect:** Regularly review your progress and celebrate your achievements.

4. Real-Life Examples of Setting and Achieving Goals

a. Personal Goal Example:

Goal: "I want to run a 5K race."

Steps:

1. **Define the Goal:** Run a 5K race.
2. **Break it Down:** Start with walking, then run short distances, gradually increasing.

3. **Set a Timeline:** Train for 3 months.
4. **Celebrate:** Reward yourself with a new running outfit or a relaxing day out after the race.

b. Professional Goal Example:

Goal: "I want to earn a promotion at work."

Steps:

1. **Define the Goal:** Get promoted to a managerial position.
2. **Break it Down:** Improve skills, take on additional responsibilities, seek feedback.
3. **Set a Timeline:** Aim for a promotion within one year.
4. **Celebrate:** Treat yourself to a special dinner or a small gift after receiving the promotion.

5. Tools and Resources for Goal Setting

a. Goal-Setting Apps

- **Trello:** A project management app for tracking tasks and goals.
- **Habitica:** A habit-building and goal-setting app with gamified features.

- **Todoist:** A task management app for setting and tracking goals.
- **GoalsOnTrack:** A goal-setting and productivity app with SMART goal features.

b. Books on Goal Setting

- **"Atomic Habits: An Easy & Proven Way to Build Good Habits & Break Bad Ones"** by James Clear.
- **"The 7 Habits of Highly Effective People: Powerful Lessons in Personal Change"** by Stephen R. Covey.
- **"Goals!: How to Get Everything You Want — Faster Than You Ever Thought Possible"** by Brian Tracy.

c. Workshops and Courses

- **Online Courses:** Platforms like Coursera, Udemy, and LinkedIn Learning offer courses on goal setting and personal development.
- **Local Workshops:** Look for workshops on goal setting at community centers or professional organizations.

Conclusion

Setting realistic goals and celebrating small victories are crucial aspects of personal growth and achievement. By understanding the characteristics of realistic goals, learning to set achievable objectives, and implementing effective strategies for celebration, you can build confidence and maintain motivation on your journey to success.

Chapter 8

Staying Patient

Introduction

Recovery from mental health challenges, personal setbacks, or significant life changes often demands a great deal of patience. Unlike linear progressions that one might find in straightforward tasks or goals, the journey to recovery is rarely a smooth, predictable path. This guide explores the concept of patience in the context of recovery, offering strategies for managing setbacks, understanding non-linear progress, and recognizing personal growth and healing over time.

1. Understanding the Non-Linear Nature of Recovery

a. What Does Non-Linear Recovery Mean?

Recovery is a complex and often unpredictable process. Unlike a straight path from problem to solution, recovery is marked by ups and downs, setbacks, and advances.

Non-linear recovery means that progress is not always steady or predictable.

Key Characteristics of Non-Linear Recovery:

- **Fluctuations:** You might experience periods of improvement followed by setbacks. For instance, feeling better one week and worse the next is a normal part of the recovery process.
- **Varied Experiences:** Different aspects of recovery might progress at different rates. For example, you might find emotional healing is moving forward faster than behavioral changes.
- **Overlaps:** Progress in one area can overlap with struggles in another. For instance, as you get better at managing stress, you might still have days where your old habits resurface.

b. The Importance of Understanding Non-Linear Recovery

Recognizing that recovery is non-linear helps you:

- **Adjust Expectations:** Set realistic expectations and understand that setbacks are part of the process.
- **Maintain Hope:** Keep faith that improvement is possible even when progress seems slow or uneven.
- **Develop Resilience:** Build resilience by accepting that challenges are part of the healing journey.

c. Examples of Non-Linear Recovery

1. Mental Health Recovery:

Someone recovering from depression might experience good days and bad days. They may see improvement in mood, only to face a temporary relapse.

2. Physical Injury Recovery:

A person recovering from a surgery might have days where they feel stronger and days where they experience pain or discomfort.

3. Personal Development:

In personal growth, one might make significant strides in self-awareness, only to encounter old habits or emotional responses.

d. The Psychological Impact of Non-Linear Recovery

Understanding that recovery isn't a straight path can help manage feelings of frustration or inadequacy. It's essential to accept that:

- **Relapses are Normal:** They do not signify failure but are a natural part of the recovery process.
- **Progress is Not Always Visible:** Sometimes you might be growing internally even if external progress isn't apparent.

2. Being Patient with Oneself

a. The Role of Self-Compassion

Self-compassion involves treating yourself with kindness and understanding during difficult times. It's crucial for maintaining patience with oneself.

Components of Self-Compassion:

- **Self-Kindness:** Speak to yourself with kindness rather than self-criticism.

- **Common Humanity:** Understand that everyone faces struggles and that you are not alone.
- **Mindfulness:** Observe your emotions and thoughts without judgment.

Strategies for Practicing Self-Compassion:

1. **Self-Talk:** Replace negative self-talk with positive affirmations.

   Example: Instead of "I'll never get better," say, "I am doing my best, and progress takes time."

2. **Forgiveness:** Forgive yourself for setbacks and mistakes.

   Example: If you had a bad day, remind yourself that it's okay and part of the process.

3. **Understanding:** Acknowledge that healing is a gradual process.

   Example: Remind yourself that improvement doesn't happen overnight.

b. Setting Realistic Expectations for Yourself

Understanding and setting realistic expectations helps maintain patience:

- **Small Steps:** Break goals into manageable steps and celebrate small achievements.

  Example: Instead of aiming to be perfectly healed, focus on making small, positive changes.

- **Flexible Timelines:** Allow yourself extra time to achieve goals.

  Example: If you don't meet a deadline, adjust your schedule rather than feeling discouraged.

c. Dealing with Self-Doubt

Self-doubt can hinder patience. Strategies for overcoming self-doubt include:

- **Challenge Negative Thoughts:** Identify and challenge irrational thoughts.

Example: "I'm not good enough" can be challenged with "I am making progress every day."

- **Seek Feedback:** Get constructive feedback from trusted sources.

  Example: Discuss your progress with a therapist or mentor for an objective perspective.

d. Embracing the Journey

See the recovery process as a journey rather than a destination. This perspective helps maintain patience:

- **Focus on Growth:** Recognize that growth happens over time.

  Example: Reflect on how far you've come rather than only focusing on where you want to be.

- **Enjoy the Process:** Find joy in small victories and the learning process.

  Example: Celebrate your efforts, not just the outcomes.

3. Recognizing Growth and Healing Over Time

a. Measuring Progress

Measuring progress can be challenging but is crucial for recognizing growth.

Methods for Measuring Progress:

1. **Journaling:** Keep a daily or weekly journal to track your thoughts, feelings, and achievements.

   Example: Write about your daily experiences and review them periodically.

2. **Progress Reviews:** Regularly review your goals and achievements.

   Example: Set monthly check-ins to evaluate your progress.

3. **Reflecting on Changes:** Look at how your thoughts, behaviors, and emotions have evolved.

   Example: Note improvements in your emotional responses or coping strategies.

b. Celebrating Small Victories

Celebrating small victories reinforces positive behaviors and acknowledges progress:

Ways to Celebrate Small Victories:

1. **Acknowledge Achievements:** Take time to recognize your accomplishments.

   Example: Celebrate completing a challenging task or reaching a milestone.

2. **Reward Yourself:** Give yourself a reward for achieving a goal.

   Example: Treat yourself to something you enjoy, like a favorite meal or a movie.

3. **Share Success:** Share your achievements with friends, family, or support groups.

   Example: Talk about your progress in a supportive environment.

c. Reflecting on Growth

Reflect on your growth to appreciate how far you've come:

Reflection Techniques:

1. **Review Your Journey:** Look back at where you started and compare it to where you are now.

   Example: Compare past journal entries to current ones to see your progress.

2. **Acknowledge Efforts:** Recognize the effort you put into your recovery.

   Example: Reflect on the challenges you faced and how you overcame them.

3. **Reevaluate Goals:** Adjust your goals based on your progress.

   Example: Set new goals that reflect your current achievements and aspirations.

d. Understanding Healing

Healing is not a destination but a process of continual growth:

- **Ongoing Process:** Accept that healing is ongoing and that there will always be opportunities for growth.

  Example: Recognize that you might continue to develop new coping strategies.

- **Adaptive Change:** Embrace changes as they come and adapt to new circumstances.

  Example: When you reach a goal, set new ones that reflect your growth.

4. Strategies for Staying Patient

a. Practicing Mindfulness

Mindfulness helps you stay focused on the present moment and manage impatience.

Mindfulness Techniques:

1. **Meditation:** Practice meditation to cultivate mindfulness.

   Example: Spend a few minutes each day meditating on your thoughts and feelings.

2. **Mindful Breathing:** Use deep breathing exercises to center yourself.

   Example: Practice deep breathing when you feel impatient or frustrated.

3. **Grounding Techniques:** Use grounding exercises to stay present.

   Example: Focus on your senses by noting what you see, hear, and feel.

b. Building a Support System

A support system provides encouragement and helps you stay patient:

Ways to Build a Support System:

1. **Seek Support:** Reach out to friends, family, or support groups.

   Example: Join a support group for shared experiences and advice.

2. **Connect Regularly:** Maintain regular contact with your support network.

Example: Schedule weekly check-ins with friends or support group members.

3. **Share Your Goals:** Talk about your goals and progress with others.

   Example: Share updates on your achievements and challenges with your support network.

c. Developing Coping Strategies

Effective coping strategies help manage frustration and maintain patience:

Coping Strategies:

1. **Stress Management:** Use stress management techniques like exercise or hobbies.

   Example: Engage in activities that help you relax and unwind.

2. **Healthy Routines:** Establish routines that promote well-being.

   Example: Develop a daily routine that includes exercise, healthy eating, and relaxation.

3. **Goal Adjustments:** Be flexible and adjust your goals as needed.

Example: Revise your goals based on your progress and current situation.

d. Setting Realistic Expectations

Set realistic expectations for your progress and growth:

Tips for Setting Expectations:

1. **Understand Limitations:** Acknowledge your limitations and work within them.

Example: Set achievable goals that align with your current abilities.

2. **Plan for Setbacks:** Expect setbacks and plan for how you will handle them.

Example: Develop a plan for managing challenges and setbacks.

3. **Focus on Effort:** Emphasize effort and perseverance rather than just outcomes.

Example: Celebrate your efforts and commitment to your goals.

5. Case Studies and Examples

a. Case Study: Overcoming Anxiety

Background: Emma struggled with severe anxiety for several years. Her journey to recovery was marked by periods of progress and setbacks.

Approach: Emma practiced mindfulness, sought therapy, and set small, achievable goals. She was patient with herself during setbacks and celebrated her achievements, such as completing therapy sessions and practicing relaxation techniques.

Outcome: Over time, Emma noticed significant improvements in her anxiety levels and developed effective coping strategies. Her patience and perseverance were key to her recovery.

b. Case Study: Recovering from a Physical Injury

Background: Mark experienced a serious knee injury that required surgery and extensive rehabilitation.

Approach: Mark followed his rehabilitation plan diligently, though he faced periods of pain and frustration. He set small goals for his recovery, such as increasing his range of motion, and celebrated each milestone.

Outcome: Mark's patience and commitment led to a successful recovery and improved physical health. He learned to manage his expectations and appreciate the slow but steady progress.

c. Case Study: Personal Growth After a Setback

Background: Sarah faced a significant career setback after being passed over for a promotion.

Approach: Sarah focused on personal growth by setting new career goals, seeking mentorship, and reflecting on her professional development. She was patient with herself as she worked through her feelings of disappointment.

Outcome: Sarah's patience and efforts led to new career opportunities and personal growth. She used the setback as a learning experience and set new, achievable goals for her future.

6. The Psychological Science Behind Patience

a. The Role of Patience in Mental Health

Patience plays a crucial role in mental health and emotional well-being:

- **Emotional Regulation:** Patience helps manage emotions and reduces frustration.

  Example: Being patient with yourself during setbacks can prevent emotional distress.

- **Resilience Building:** Patience fosters resilience by helping you cope with challenges.

  Example: Patiently working through difficulties builds emotional strength.

b. Psychological Theories on Patience

1. **Cognitive Behavioral Theory:** This theory suggests that changing negative thought patterns can improve patience.

Example: Cognitive restructuring techniques help you manage impatience.

2. **Mindfulness-Based Stress Reduction:** Mindfulness techniques promote patience and acceptance.

    Example: Mindfulness practices reduce stress and increase patience.

c. Research on Patience and Well-being

Studies show that patience is linked to better mental health outcomes:

- **Studies:** Research indicates that patience is associated with lower levels of stress and improved emotional well-being.

  Example: A study found that patients who practiced patience reported better mental health.

- **Implications:** Understanding these findings reinforces the value of patience in personal growth and recovery.

7. Resources for Building Patience

a. Books on Patience and Resilience

- **"The Gifts of Imperfection: Let Go of Who You Think You're Supposed to Be and Embrace Who You Are"** by Brené Brown.
- **"The Power of Now: A Guide to Spiritual Enlightenment"** by Eckhart Tolle.
- **"Resilient: How to Grow an Unshakable Core of Calm, Strength, and Happiness"** by Rick Hanson.

b. Online Resources and Apps

- **Headspace:** Meditation and mindfulness app for building patience and managing stress.
- **Calm:** App for meditation, sleep, and relaxation to promote patience and emotional well-being.
- **Insight Timer:** Meditation app with guided sessions for patience and mindfulness.

c. Support Groups and Forums

- **Mental Health Forums:** Online communities for sharing experiences and advice.

- **Support Groups:** Local or online groups for specific mental health issues or personal growth.

Conclusion

Patience is a vital component of the recovery process. Understanding that recovery is non-linear, being patient with oneself, and recognizing growth and healing over time are essential for achieving long-term success. This guide has explored various aspects of patience, including its role in the recovery process, strategies for maintaining patience, and ways to celebrate progress.

This guide provides a comprehensive look at the role of patience in the recovery process, offering strategies, insights, and practical tools to support your journey toward healing and growth.

Feel free to adjust and expand upon these sections based on specific experiences or additional insights you might have.

Chapter 9

Conclusion

1. Reflecting on the Transformative Experience of Overcoming Depression

Overcoming depression is a profound and transformative journey that reshapes one's understanding of self, life, and the future. This section reflects on the deeply personal and often arduous process of navigating through depression, highlighting the pivotal moments, lessons learned, and growth experienced along the way.

a. The Journey from Darkness to Light

Depression can feel like being trapped in an unending night, where hope seems distant, and every day is a struggle. Yet, the journey through depression is not merely about reaching the other side but about the personal transformation that occurs along the way.

1. Acknowledging the Depths of Despair

The first step in overcoming depression involves recognizing and accepting the profound despair and hopelessness that characterizes the condition. This phase is marked by:

- **Emotional Turmoil:** Facing intense feelings of sadness, worthlessness, and disconnection.
- **Physical Symptoms:** Experiencing fatigue, changes in sleep patterns, and loss of appetite.
- **Mental Challenges:** Battling intrusive negative thoughts and cognitive distortions.

Reflecting on this initial phase reveals that the process of overcoming depression often begins with the acceptance of these emotions as valid and real. For many, it is a time of deep introspection and grappling with one's mental state.

2. The Path to Recovery

Recovery from depression is not a sudden or magical transformation but a gradual process of reclaiming one's life. Key moments in this transformative journey include:

- **Seeking Help:** The decision to reach out for professional support can be a turning point. Recognizing that depression is a medical condition rather than a personal failing is crucial.

Example: The moment when you reach out to a therapist or counselor signifies the beginning of the healing process. It marks the transition from isolation to seeking support.

- **Embracing Therapy:** Engaging with therapy offers a structured space for exploring thoughts and emotions. It introduces new coping mechanisms and insights into one's mental health.

Example: The experience of discovering that talking about your feelings can lead to emotional relief and a deeper understanding of oneself.

- **The Role of Medication:** For some, medication becomes a necessary part of managing depression. Understanding the benefits and limitations of antidepressants helps in adjusting expectations and maintaining hope.

Example: The realization that medication can stabilize mood and make other forms of therapy more effective.

3. Finding Strength in Small Victories

Throughout the recovery process, celebrating small victories is essential for maintaining motivation and acknowledging progress. These victories might seem minor but represent significant steps forward in the journey of healing.

- **Daily Achievements:** Recognizing that even small actions, such as getting out of bed or engaging in a hobby, are significant achievements.

  Example: Successfully completing a daily routine or managing to attend therapy sessions.

- **Personal Growth:** Reflecting on how overcoming depression has led to personal growth, such as increased resilience, greater empathy, and a renewed sense of purpose.

  Example: Gaining a deeper appreciation for life and understanding that overcoming depression has made you stronger and more compassionate.

b. Lessons Learned from the Experience

The experience of overcoming depression teaches valuable life lessons:

1. **The Value of Self-Compassion:** Learning to be kind to oneself in the face of adversity.
    - **Example:** Realizing that self-compassion involves forgiving oneself for setbacks and acknowledging that growth takes time.
2. **The Importance of Seeking Help:** Understanding that reaching out for professional support is not a weakness but a crucial step towards recovery.
    - **Example:** Learning that asking for help can open doors to resources and support that make recovery possible.
3. **The Power of Patience:** Recognizing that recovery is a slow and often uneven process.
    - **Example:** Accepting that healing takes time and that it's

okay to have setbacks along the way.

c. The Ongoing Nature of Healing

Overcoming depression is not an end but a beginning of a new phase in life. Healing is an ongoing process that involves continual self-care, growth, and adaptation.

- **Future Focus:** Embracing the journey of continued personal development and emotional health.

  Example: Setting future goals for continued personal growth and well-being.

- **Long-Term Strategies:** Maintaining practices that support mental health, such as mindfulness, therapy, and self-compassion.

  Example: Continuing to use coping strategies learned during recovery to manage future challenges.

2. Emphasizing the Importance of Seeking Help and Having a Strong Support System

a. The Necessity of Professional Help

Seeking professional help is a critical step in overcoming depression. It involves acknowledging that mental health conditions require specialized support and that professional guidance can make a significant difference.

1. Why Professional Help is Essential

- **Expert Guidance:** Therapists and counselors offer professional insights and techniques for managing depression.

  Example: Professionals provide cognitive-behavioral strategies and therapeutic techniques that are proven to help manage and overcome depression.

- **Structured Support:** Therapy provides a structured environment for exploring mental health issues.

  Example: Regular sessions with a therapist offer a consistent space for discussing feelings and developing coping strategies.

- **Medical Intervention:** For some, medication is a necessary component of treatment.

  Example: Antidepressants can help manage chemical imbalances in the brain, making other forms of therapy more effective.

2. Finding the Right Therapist

Choosing the right mental health professional is crucial for effective treatment:

- **Qualifications:** Look for licensed professionals with experience in treating depression.

  Example: Researching qualifications and reading reviews can help find a therapist who fits your needs.

- **Compatibility:** It's important to find a therapist with whom you feel comfortable.

  Example: The first few sessions can help determine if you feel understood and supported.

b. Building a Strong Support System

A support system includes friends, family, and support groups who provide emotional and practical support during recovery.

1. The Role of Friends and Family

- **Emotional Support:** Loved ones offer comfort, encouragement, and a sense of connection.

  Example: Talking to a friend or family member about your struggles can provide relief and support.

- **Practical Help:** Support from loved ones can include practical assistance, such as helping with daily tasks.

  Example: A family member helping with chores or offering to accompany you to appointments.

2. The Benefits of Support Groups

Support groups provide a sense of community and shared experience:

- **Shared Experiences:** Meeting others who understand what you're going through can be comforting.

Example: Hearing others' stories in a support group can provide hope and insight.

- **Collective Wisdom:** Support groups offer a space to share coping strategies and advice.

  Example: Gaining new perspectives and techniques from group members.

3. Building and Maintaining Your Support Network

- **Reaching Out:** Actively seeking and maintaining connections with supportive individuals.

  Example: Regularly scheduling time to connect with friends and family.

- **Being Open:** Sharing your feelings and needs with your support network.

  Example: Being honest about your struggles and what kind of support you need.

3. Encouragement for Others Struggling with Depression

a. Reassurance for Those Facing Depression

For those currently struggling with depression, it's important to offer hope and encouragement.

1. The Promise of Recovery

- **Hope for the Future:** Emphasize that recovery is possible, even if it doesn't feel that way right now.

  Example: Sharing stories of individuals who have successfully navigated depression and found joy in life again.

- **Progress is Possible:** Reinforce that improvement is gradual and achievable.

  Example: Remind yourself that every small step forward counts and contributes to long-term recovery.

2. Encouragement to Seek Help

- **Taking the First Step:** Encourage seeking professional help as a courageous and essential step.

Example: Reiterate that asking for help is a sign of strength, not weakness.

- **Accessing Resources:** Suggest reaching out to therapists, support groups, and other resources.

Example: Provide information about finding a therapist or joining a support group.

b. Building Patience and Resilience

1. Patience in the Process

- **Understanding the Journey:** Emphasize that recovery is a process that takes time.

Example: Encourage accepting the slow pace of recovery and focusing on small victories.

- **Resilience:** Teach the value of resilience in facing challenges.

Example: Share techniques for building resilience, such as mindfulness and positive self-talk.

2. Embracing Growth

- **Recognizing Personal Growth:** Encourage recognizing and valuing personal growth that occurs during recovery.

  Example: Reflect on how facing and overcoming depression can lead to personal development.

- **Future Possibilities:** Inspire hope for a fulfilling future beyond depression.

  Example: Share examples of how recovery can lead to new opportunities and a more meaningful life.

4. Practical Tips for Those Struggling with Depression

a. Developing Coping Strategies

1. Daily Self-Care

- **Routine:** Establishing a daily routine can provide structure and a sense of normalcy.

Example: Create a daily schedule that includes time for self-care, work, and leisure.

- **Healthy Habits:** Incorporate healthy habits such as regular exercise, balanced diet, and sufficient sleep.

Example: Develop a self-care routine that includes physical activity, nutritious meals, and relaxation.

2. Mindfulness and Relaxation Techniques

- **Mindfulness Practices:** Engage in mindfulness practices to manage stress and emotions.

Example: Practice mindfulness meditation, deep breathing, or yoga.

- **Relaxation Techniques:** Use techniques for relaxation and stress reduction.

Example: Try guided imagery, progressive muscle relaxation, or journaling.

b. Seeking Professional Support

1. Finding a Therapist

- **Research:** Look for qualified mental health professionals in your area.

  Example: Use online directories or ask for referrals from trusted sources.

- **First Steps:** Schedule an initial consultation to see if the therapist is a good fit.

  Example: Prepare questions for your first meeting to assess compatibility.

2. Joining Support Groups

- **Local and Online Groups:** Find support groups in your community or online.

  Example: Look for local meetups or online forums for mental health support.

- **Participating in Groups:** Engage actively in group discussions and activities.

  Example: Share your experiences and listen to others in the group.

5. Final Words of Encouragement

Overcoming depression is a challenging but achievable goal. The journey involves facing difficult truths, seeking help, and building a supportive network. It requires patience, resilience, and a willingness to embrace the process of recovery.

a. Embracing Hope

No matter how dark things may seem, there is always hope for a better future. Recovery is possible, and every effort made towards healing is a step in the right direction.

- **Words of Hope:** Encourage others to believe in their ability to overcome depression.

  Example: "Even in the darkest moments, there is hope for a brighter tomorrow."

b. The Importance of Persistence

Recovery requires persistence and dedication. It's important to stay committed to the process, even when progress feels slow.

- **Staying Committed:** Reinforce the importance of persistence in the recovery process.

  Example: "Keep moving forward, one step at a time. Each step brings you closer to healing."

c. The Power of Community

Finally, remember that you are not alone. There is a community of individuals who understand and support you.

- **Finding Connection:** Emphasize the strength found in community and shared experiences.

  Example: "Reach out for support and remember that there are people who care and understand what you're going through."

6. Conclusion

The journey of overcoming depression is both personal and universal. It is a path marked by struggle, growth, and transformation. By reflecting on the experience, emphasizing the importance of professional help and support, and offering encouragement to others, we acknowledge the complexity of the recovery process and the hope that it offers.

a. Summary of Key Points

- **Transformative Experience:** Reflecting on how overcoming depression changes one's life and perspective.
- **Seeking Help:** The necessity of professional support and building a strong support system.
- **Encouragement:** Offering hope and practical advice for others struggling with depression.
- **Practical Strategies:** Providing tips for managing depression and maintaining mental health.
- **Final Encouragement:** Inspiring resilience, hope, and community support in the face of depression.

b. Final Encouragement

As you navigate your own journey through depression, remember that you have the strength within you to overcome it. Seek help, lean on your support network, and be patient with yourself. Your path to recovery is a testament to your resilience and your hope for a brighter future.

Words of Wisdom: "Your struggle does not define you. Your strength and perseverance do. Keep moving forward, and know that you are not alone."

By embracing these insights and strategies, you can find hope, healing, and a renewed sense of purpose as you continue your journey towards mental well-being.